BRITISH RAILWAYS

PAST and PRESENT

No 38

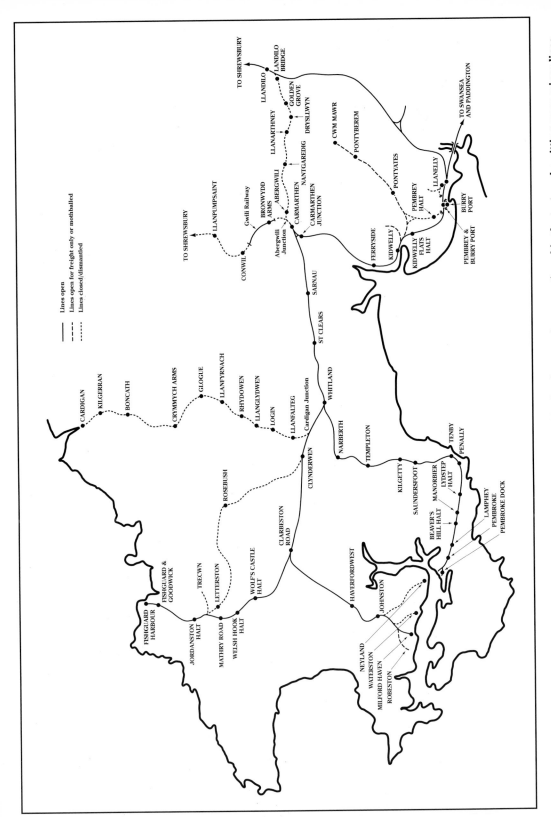

Map of the area covered by this book, showing only the locations featured in the photographs or mentioned in the text, and omitting some minor lines.

BRITISH RAILWAYS

PAST and PRESENT

No 38
West Wales

Terry Gough

Past and Present

Past & Present Publishing Ltd

First published in 2002

British Library Cataloguing in Publication Data

A catalogue record for this book is available from the British Library.

ISBN 1 85895 175 5

Past & Present Publishing Ltd
The Trundle
Ringstead Road
Great Addington
Kettering
Northants NN14 4BW

Tel/Fax: 01536 330588
email: sales@nostalgiacollection.com
Website: www.nostalgiacollection.com

All tickets and other items of ephemera are from the author's collection.

Printed and bound in Great Britain

BIBLIOGRAPHY

Barrie, D. S. M. *A Regional History of the Railways of Great Britain, Volume 12 South Wales* (David St John Thomas, 1994) ISBN 0 946537 69 0

Clinker, C. R. *Register of Closed Passenger Stations and Goods Depots* (Avon-Anglia Publications and Services, 1978) ISBN 0 905466 19 5

Cooke, R. A. *Track Plans of the GWR and BR(W), Sections 57 Llanelly and 58 West Wales*

Gough, Terry *British Railways Past and Present No 37: South Wales Part 3* (Past & Present Publishing, 2002) ISBN 1 85895 162 3

Hale, Michael *Steam in South Wales, Volume 2 North and West of Swansea* (OPC, 1981) ISBN 86093 152 8

Morris, J. P. *The Pembroke & Tenby Railway* (Laidlaw-Burgess, 1976)

Page, James *Forgotten Railways: South Wales* (David & Charles, 1988)

Price, M. R. C. *The Llanelly & Mynydd Mawr Railway* (Oakwood Press, 1992) ISBN 0 85361 423 7

The Gwendraeth Valleys Railway (Oakwood Press, 1997) ISBN 0 85361 505 5

The Pembroke & Tenby Railway (Oakwood Press, 1986) ISBN 0 85361 327 3

The Saundersfoot Railway (Oakwood Press, 1989) ISBN 0 85361 382 6

Price, M. R. C. *The Whitland & Cardigan Railway* (Oakwood Press, 1991) ISBN 0 85361 409 1

Siviter, Roger *British Railways Past and Present No 32: Mid Wales and the Marches* (Past & Present Publishing, 1998) ISBN 1 85895 137 2

Smith, Paul *The Handbook of Steam Motive Power Depots, Volume 2* (Platform 5 Publishing Ltd, 1989) ISBN 0 906579 95 3

(65) R. & S. B. R.

Carmarthen Town, G.W.R.

Via Briton Ferry.

CONTENTS

ACKNOWLEDGEMENTS

I greatly appreciate the willingness of other photographers to loan me material for this book. I also thank Ray Caston of the Welsh Railways Research Circle for his help. Some of the closed stations are on private property and I am grateful to the various owners for granting access; without their help some of the 'past and present' comparisons would not have been possible. My wife accompanied me on one of the visits to West Wales (May 2000), but opted out of the several subsequent trips. I am grateful for her wisdom on both counts.

CRYMMYCH ARMS station was on the Cardigan branch. Class 4500 No 4557 pauses with the 4.00pm from Whitland on 9 June 1960. The station area is still in use, as shown in the view taken from the same point on 15 May 2000. *Hugh Ballantyne/TG*

INTRODUCTION

I lived for a short while in Haverfordwest, but this was when I was a child and some years before I had a camera and developed an interest in railways. In preparing this book I have therefore had to rely on the generosity of other photographers in providing me with the 'past' material, my only contribution being a photograph that I took in 1954 at Burry Port.

In the course of taking the 'present' photographs I made several visits to West Wales. Returning after such a long time was an interesting experience, particularly as so much has changed both on the railways and in the towns. My memory of past events was occasionally jogged and I recalled in particular a bus journey made toward the end of the Second World War from Milford Haven to Neyland on an ancient vehicle barely able to climb the hills. I made the same bus journey in October 2001, having arrived at Milford Haven by train. I was able to continue beyond Neyland over the river bridge that had subsequently been built, to catch a train from Pembroke. For other stations still open I also made the 'present' visits by train wherever possible. For the closed stations I had no choice but to use my car (manufactured in 1966), as many are in isolated locations with infrequent or no bus services.

Changes have even took place during the period over which I took the 'present' photographs. From the photographer's point of view a particularly unwelcome development has been the erection of intrusive high-security railings at several places, in particular at Haverfordwest and Milford Haven. The other change has been the loss of the train operating franchise by Wales & West. In October 2001 I caught a train to Carmarthen marked 'Wessex Trains'.

The Great Western Railway (GWR) main line from South Wales to Carmarthen opened in October 1852 and was converted from broad gauge to standard gauge 20 years later. The first Carmarthen station was located at what subsequently became Carmarthen Junction, a mile south of the town. When the line to Conwil (and eventually Aberystwyth) was opened in 1860, a station was built on the edge of the town; this was re-sited in 1902 and all main-line trains (except boat trains) were routed via the town with a reversal before proceeding east or west, a practice that continues to the present day. There are currently proposals to re-site the station again. Junction station closed in 1926. The Aberystwyth line closed in 1973, but a short section from Bronwydd Arms north toward Conwil was reopened for passengers in 1978 by the Gwili Railway. In March 2001 services were extended, giving the railway an operating distance of just over 2 miles.

The London & North Western Railway (LNWR) reached Carmarthen in 1864 via a line from Llandilo, although there were no through trains to North West England, a change at Llandilo being necessary. The line closed completely in 1963.

Haverfordwest was reached in 1854 and Neyland (then known as New Milford) two years later. This was a major port with sailings to Ireland, but it lost its importance once a new line to Fishguard was opened, and it eventually closed in 1964. A branch was built to Milford Haven in 1863 and this became the main line once Neyland lost the Irish traffic. Several oil refineries and storage depots with rail links were later built in the Milford Haven area, but oil traffic has dropped dramatically in recent years and the branch to Waterston is not currently in use. Only the Robeston branch has a regular oil train, but this runs less frequently than even a year ago.

Railway building was also taking place between Pembroke and Tenby, this isolated line being opened in 1863 and extended to Pembroke Dock the following year. The line was extended north-east in 1866 to Whitland, where the company had a station adjacent to the main line; at the same time a new station was built at Tenby. After the GWR abandoned the broad gauge, trains from Pembroke used the main station at Whitland. A goods-only extension from the terminus at Pembroke Dock into the dockyard was opened in 1871, but was out of use by the 1960s and buffer stops have been erected at Pembroke Dock station. Another short branch ran just east of Pembroke Dock station to Hobbs Point, but this too was abandoned by the 1960s. It seems odd that there was no passenger service on this branch, as there was a ferry from Hobbs Point to Neyland. With the introduction of 'railmotors', several halts were added to the line, all of which are now closed.

In the Saundersfoot area there were several industries, including coalmining. These were served by a railway that had exchange sidings with the Whitland to Pembroke line. The Saundersfoot Railway was never absorbed into the GWR and closed in 1939.

In 1876 a line was opened from the main line just west of Clynderwen to Rosebush, mainly to serve the slate quarries. It closed at the end of 1882, re-opened two years later and closed for the second time in 1888. It opened again in 1895 with a passenger service to Letterston, which was extended to Fishguard & Goodwick in 1899. Another line, with easier gradients, was later opened to Fishguard Harbour and this ran north from Clarbeston Road to join the Letterston line 5 miles from Fishguard. The Letterston line closed during the First World War, later re-opened, but lost its passenger service for the last time in 1937. Also in 1937 a short branch was built from the northern end of the Letterston line to Trecwn for military traffic. The Letterston line closed completely as far as Letterston in 1949 and north from Letterston in 1965, apart from the final half mile, which was retained for Trecwn trains until this closed in 1995.

The branch from Whitland to Cardigan opened as far as Glogue in 1875 for goods, to serve the slate quarry and the lead and silver mines at Llanfyrnach. It was extended to Crymmych Arms for passengers in 1875 and reached Cardigan in 1886. Unfortunately for the line, the mines closed in 1891 and the quarry in 1926. There was still plenty of general goods traffic, but both this and passenger numbers dwindled over the years to unacceptably low levels. Passenger services were withdrawn in September 1962 and goods services in May 1963. The track was lifted the following year.

East of Carmarthen there were two branch lines, both built predominantly for coal traffic. The Gwendraeth Valley Railway was 2 miles long and ran from Kidwelly to Mynydd-y-Garreg. There was never a public passenger service, and the line closed in 1960, although it was later re-opened, then mothballed. Another line, the Burry Port & Gwendraeth Valley Railway, opened in 1869 to Cwm Mawr to carry coal and minerals. It officially began a passenger service between Burry Port and Pontyberem in 1909, which was extended to Cwm Mawr in 1913. Passenger services ceased in September 1953, although the line continued to be used by coal trains for many years and the track is still in place.

The railways of West Wales have not suffered as much as other parts of Wales. There are still services from Carmarthen and points west to Pembroke Dock, Milford Haven and Fishguard Harbour. One closed station has been re-opened and many stations have become request stops. Even from these there are through trains to and from Swansea and more distant destinations including Manchester Piccadilly, Portsmouth Harbour and Waterloo, but not Paddington, which is served by two trains per day from Carmarthen. Fishguard Harbour has two boat trains per day, but all intermediate stations from Clarbeston Road are closed. Tourist leaflets are available on the Pembroke Coast line with a short description of each town served by the railway and various walks from the stations; in addition, various Freedom of Wales passes are available, which can be used on the trains and some buses.

I have used the placename spellings as in the Western Region Passenger Services Timetable of September 1961, or earlier in cases where stations had already been closed.

Terry Gough
Sherborne, Dorset

8

Carmarthen to Pembroke Dock

CARMARTHEN (1): The station is at the north-eastern point of a triangle formed by the lines from Swansea, Whitland and Aberystwyth. On 8 August 1962 an Aberystwyth train leaves in the hands of 43XX Class No 7318. On the extreme left is the GWR locomotive depot.

A visit on 18 May 2000 revealed several significant changes to the station. The footbridge and all buildings on the island platform have been removed. On the other side the canopy is intact, but a new flat-roofed building has replaced an older structure. Closure of the line to Aberystwyth resulted in the lifting of the track behind the camera, and to this extent Carmarthen has become a terminus, with trains from Swansea and other points east reversing here en route to Whitland and beyond, and vice versa. On 20 September 2001 Class 158 No 158871 forms the 05.46 Gloucester to Milford Haven service, which is allowed 3 minutes for reversing.
C. J. Gammell/TG

CARMARTHEN (2): The same location can be viewed from the adjacent road bridge. In May 1958 'Hall' Class No 6905 *Claughton Hall*, recently arrived from Swansea, takes the first two coaches of its train out of the station.

Today Carmarthen has only two through trains to Paddington (three in mid-summer), one of which leaves at 02.40. This leaves the 07.35 as the only realistic option to photograph, and it is seen here in September 2001 alongside the 07.30 service to Milford Haven worked by Class 150 No 150253. *Norman Simmons, courtesy Hugh Davies/TG*

CARMARTHEN (3): A member of the 16XX Class acts as station pilot on 8 July 1950. In the same position 51 years later is the 12.16 service from Pembroke Dock, consisting of Class 153 No 153312. After reversing, the train will continue to Swansea, arriving at 14.20. *R. S. Carpenter/TG*

CARMARTHEN (4): The 6.55am from Aberystwyth has just arrived at Carmarthen behind 2251 Class No 2298 on 12 September 1952. The 'present' view shows the bare island platform, while in the main platform is Class 158 No 158871. *R. J. Buckley, courtesy Don Gatehouse/TG*

CARMARTHEN GWR LOCOMOTIVE DEPOT, code 87G in BR days, is seen on 20 September 1962. It closed two years later, and has since been demolished and most of the track removed. The site was derelict in September 2000, but by the following September it was in use by a railway maintenance company, as shown here. *R. S. Carpenter/TG*

CARMARTHEN LNWR LOCOMOTIVE DEPOT: The LNWR ran trains between Carmarthen and Llandilo, where there were connections to the north. The LNWR also had a locomotive shed at Carmarthen and this was located a little to the north of the station. The 'past' photograph shows the site (to the left) on 21 September 1962. The lines from Llandilo and Aberystwyth diverge a mile to the north-east at Abergwili Junction.

In the present-day photograph the Carmarthen bypass can be seen, but the site remains identifiable. *R. S. Carpenter/TG*

SARNAU was the first station travelling west from Carmarthen, and it is seen here on 6 June 1963 as an unidentified train heads for Whitland. The station closed on 15 June the following year and no trace remains today. *Adrian Vaughan/TG*

ST CLEARS (1): This station closed to passengers on the same date, but remained open for goods until May 1966. The down 'Pembroke Coast Express' behind 43XX Class No 7321 runs into the station on 8 July 1958, where it will make a scheduled stop. The May 2000 photograph shows the same location. *R. M. Casserley/TG*

ST CLEARS (2): This is the station seen from the level crossing looking towards Carmarthen, also on 8 July 1958. The buildings and platforms have since been demolished, to leave an uninspiring view. *R. M. Casserley/TG*

WHITLAND LOCOMOTIVE DEPOT is seen, looking east, on 9 June 1960. In the foreground is 45XX Class No 5520, and the 57XX Class pannier tanks are Nos 3657 and 8738. Nothing remains of the shed today, although some of the track has been retained and is still in use. *Hugh Ballantyne/TG*

20

WHITLAND (I): Approaching the station from the east, Class 9F No 92247 is working the 9.10am from Birmingham Snow Hill to Pembroke Dock on 22 August 1959.

The factory has since expanded and a replacement signal box has been built on the opposite side of the line. The carriage sidings have gone, as has the line giving access to the outer face of the down platform and its associated level crossing. *R. O. Tuck, courtesy Don Gatehouse/TG*

WHITLAND (2): The two 'past' views show the down bay. On 12 September 1952 the 6.20pm to Cardigan is hauled by 16XX Class No 1628; the engine shed lies to the right. On 22 August 1959 the 4.00pm to Cardigan is worked by 45XX Class No 4558.

There are no longer any trains to Cardigan, but the lines to Pembroke, Milford Haven and Fishguard are still open. On 19 May 2000 the 16.05 Swansea to Pembroke Dock service is operated by Class 143 railbus No 143620.
H. C. Casserley/R. O. Tuck, courtesy Don Gatehouse/TG

NARBERTH (1): Immediately beyond Whitland the Pembroke Dock line diverges, and the first station on this line is Narberth, which is being approached by 57XX Class No 4699 heading for Pembroke Dock in July 1961.

The present-day service is operated by Class 158 and other modern DMUs. On 16 May 2000 No 158864 works the 16.05 service from Swansea, an interesting contrast with the stock used three days later (see previous page).
R. Griffiths/TG

NARBERTH (2): The 'Pembroke Coast Express' is seen at Narberth in May 1961, hauled by 'Manor' Class No 7825 *Lechlade Manor.* This train left Pembroke Dock at 1.05pm and after Whitland called only at Carmarthen, Llanelly, Swansea, Cardiff and Newport. It then ran fast to Paddington, arriving at 7.45pm.

There is now only a single line through Narberth, and the former goods yard has been given over to the storage and sale of farm machinery. The former goods shed is still in use. *R. Griffiths/TG*

TEMPLETON: 57XX Class No 4107 waits at Templeton with a Pembroke-bound goods train in August 1961. The station closed in June 1964, the goods yard having closed the previous December. All that remains today is part of the platform, as seen in May 2000. *R. Griffiths/TG*

KILGETTY (1): The station is seen looking towards the end of the line on 8 July 1958. The station is still open today, but has lost its original building. In common with Narberth and some of the stations further along the line, it is a request stop. *R. M. Casserley/TG*

KILGETTY (2): The down 'Pembroke Coast Express' enters Kilgetty on 8 July 1958. Despite its name, this train stopped at all stations between Whitland and Pembroke Dock except Beavers Hill Halt. On this occasion the engine is 43XX Class No 7321. *R. M. Casserley/TG*

SAUNDERSFOOT (1): In the spring of 1961 56XX Class No 6650 is on a train bound for Pembroke Dock. A visit in 2000 found that the up line had been removed and the platform was overgrown. On the down side all the buildings have gone, but the station is still open. Class 158 No 158834 leaves as the 09.12 Pembroke Dock to Manchester Piccadilly service on 17 May 2000. Even in winter there are two trains a day to Manchester, and one to Warminster – hardly a major destination. *R. Griffiths/TG*

SAUNDERSFOOT (2): A train from Pembroke Dock hauled by a 57XX Class pannier tank enters Saundersfoot in May 1961. The present view is much more restricted, as seen on 17 May 2000, with the Manchester train approaching. *R. Griffiths/TG*

TENBY: Seen from the footbridge on 7 July 1958 is the 5.54pm from Whitland and, approaching the station, the 6.15pm from Pembroke Dock to Swansea, double-headed by 51XX Class No 4169 and 43XX Class No 7340.

The view from this point is still impressive, despite the embankment being partly obscured. One train a day currently terminates here, rather than running right through to Pembroke Dock. *R. M. Casserley/TG*

A further view of Tenby station as a goods train from Pembroke Dock arrives behind 45XX Class No 5549 in about 1960. *R. S. Carpenter*

G.W.R.

TENBY

Opposite PENALLY is a single-platform station with no passing loop. It closed in 1964, but re-opened for the summer months from 1970; it is now open all year. Apart from the usual loss of buildings, it has changed little over the 40 years separating these two photographs. The station building is now a private residence. The present-day photograph even shows a 1960s car, appropriately parked by a 'Save-a-Can' skip! *R. S. Carpenter/TG*

LYDSTEP HALT was only 1½ miles from Penally and closed at the beginning of 1956. It had first closed in 1914, but was re-opened in 1923. Little remains today other than the former station path, remnants of the platform and the milepost. *Lens of Sutton/TG*

MANORBIER is seen here on 7 July 1958, and is still open today, served by all trains on a request basis. Surprisingly, it still has its main station building and only the canopy and signal box have been removed, the latter replaced by a waiting shelter. The level crossing is now ungated and warning lights are operated by the train crew. *R. M. Casserley/TG*

BEAVER'S HILL HALT (1): In BR days this halt had a train from Whitland that stopped only on Fridays, while on Wednesdays and Saturdays a train called to set down only. In the other direction one train called daily. It is therefore perhaps no wonder that the halt closed with effect from 15 June 1964. *Lens of Sutton/TG*

BEAVER'S HILL HALT (2): The adjacent crossing was guarded by rope on this 1960s visit. It is now unguarded and all trains make a mandatory stop before crossing the road. *Lens of Sutton/TG*

LAMPHEY was another small station serving an adjacent village. In May 1961 the up 'Pembroke Coast Express' approaches the station, while in May 2000 there are no passengers for the DMU expected from Pembroke Dock within the next few minutes. *R. Griffiths/TG*

PEMBROKE was another single-platform station, conveniently situated at the eastern end of the town. The 1960s photograph shows an active goods yard, the site of which has since been used as a car park. The present-day station is simple, but smartly kept. On 20 September 2001 Class 153 No 153312 leaves as the 10.05 service from **Swansea.** *Lens of Sutton/TG*

PEMBROKE DOCK (1): There were two halts, named Golden Hill and Llanion, situated between Pembroke and Pembroke Dock stations, and these closed in 1940 and 1908 respectively. Pembroke Dock had long platforms to accommodate the long-distance trains, and in the first photograph, dated June 1958, 43XX Class No 5357 is ready to leave with the 'Pembroke Coast Express'.

There was plenty of variety on the Pembroke Dock trains. On 12 September 1952, the date of the second view, the 3.55pm to Whitland is worked by 94XX Class No 9452.

On 8 June 1960 45XX Class No 5520 is on the 3.50pm to Whitland. This platform still exists, but the trains are much shorter today. On 17 May 2000 single-car Class 153 unit No 153374 is dwarfed by the length of the platform as it waits to operate the 12.16 service to Swansea. *R. Griffiths/R. J. Buckley, courtesy Don Gatehouse/Hugh Ballantyne/TG*

PEMBROKE DOCK (2): 45XX Class No 4594 waits with a train from Whitland in June 1958. Although this is the passenger terminus, the track continued into the dock.

The present-day photograph shows Class 153 No 153374 again, having just arrived with the 10.05 service from Swansea. This really is the end of the line now and the buffer stops are just behind the camera, the line into the dock having been lifted in 1969. *R. Griffiths/TG*

PEMBROKE DOCK (3): This July 1962 view of the exterior of Pembroke Dock station shows an attractive stone building, and it was pleasing to find that this had survived and was still in good order in the spring of 2000.
R. Griffiths/TG

PEMBROKE DOCK LOCOMOTIVE DEPOT was a sub-shed of Neyland, and is seen here from a passing train on 8 June 1960. The shed closed in September 1963, and although it has been demolished the site can be identified by reference to the houses in the background. *Hugh Ballantyne/TG*

Whitland to Milford Haven and Neyland

CLYNDERWEN is the first station beyond Whitland on the main line. It was called Narberth Road until 1875, several years after the opening of a station much nearer Narberth on the Pembroke Dock line. An up train in the hands of an unidentified 'Hall' Class enters the station in July 1961. Note the height of the wooden-post signal, enabling it to be seen above the bridge on which the photographer is standing, and the smaller ringed arm guarding the down loop.

As usual the station buildings have been removed, but there is still double track. On 16 May 2000 the 08.35 Milford Haven to Swansea service is formed of two single-coach units of Class 153, the leading unit being No 153303. *R. Griffiths/TG*

CLARBESTON ROAD (1): This is the junction for Fishguard. On 8 July 1958 57XX Class No 8739 has just worked the 2.10pm from Fishguard Harbour, and is waiting to connect with a semi-fast train to Paddington, while the return working to Fishguard will connect with an express from Paddington.

The station is open as a request stop, and the bay platform still exists, but there is no track. In May 2000 Class 158 No 158864 leaves Clarbeston Road for Milford Haven. *H. C. Casserley/TG*

CLARBESTON ROAD (2): Fishguard trains sometimes departed from the down main platform, and this was the case with the 3.35pm on 11 June 1960. The train is headed by 57XX Class pannier tank No 9666.

On 16 May 2000 Class 158 No 158864 enters the station forming the 05.46 service from Gloucester. This calls at every station on the entire route except Gowerton, arriving at Milford Haven at 10.07. *Mike Vinten/TG*

CLARBESTON ROAD (3): An up fish train hauled by 43XX Class No 7306 approaches Clarbeston Road on 11 June 1960. In the background are the signals controlling the junction of the Milford Haven and Fishguard lines, with the signals cleared for the Milford Haven direction.

A clearer view of the junction, now simplified, is available in the present-day photograph. The signal box is still open. The Milford Haven line can be seen bearing left after the convergence of the two running lines through the station. *Mike Vinten/TG*

HAVERFORDWEST: The best view of the station is from the nearby goods yard road entrance. On 7 September 1983 Class 33 No 33022 works the 08.27 train from Milford Haven to Swansea. This locomotive was at the time allocated to Eastleigh and presumably had reached Pembrokeshire after hauling a Portsmouth to Cardiff train.

On 16 May 2000 Class 158 No 158843 of Cardiff Canton Depot constitutes the 16.28 service from Milford Haven to Swansea. Most trains normally use the former up platform, although the down platform is still open. Haverfordwest has won several awards, including the Anglo Irish Best Station Award in 1992. The station was refurbished in 2002 and officially re-opened on 25 April. *Hugh Ballantyne/TG*

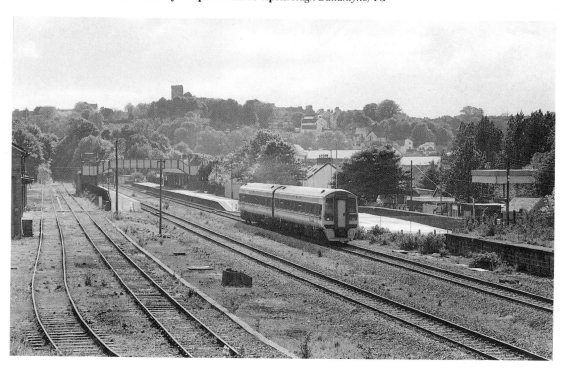

JOHNSTON was the junction station for a short (4-mile) branch to Milford Haven, the line to Neyland being regarded as more important. In the early 1950s 57XX Class pannier tank No 9652 works the Milford Haven branch. Despite this, it is the Neyland line that has closed, which took place in 1964.

There is now a single line through Johnston, occupied on 17 May 2000 by the 13.23 service from Milford Haven to Exeter St David's, worked by Class 158 unit No 158822. A new main road bridge has been built over the railway.
R. S. Carpenter/TG

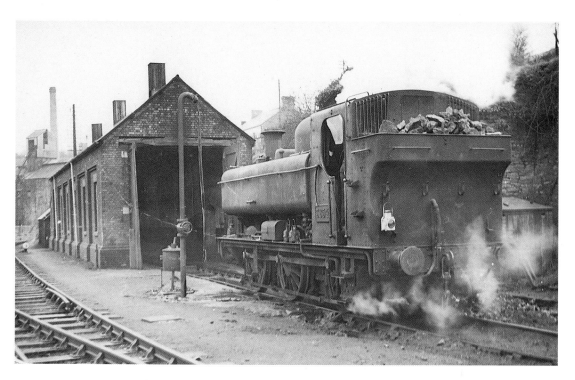

MILFORD HAVEN LOCOMOTIVE DEPOT was a sub-shed of Neyland, and was located adjacent to the station. On 5 April 1958 57XX Class No 3654 stands outside the shed. The shed closed at the end of 1962 and has been demolished, but some of the track remains. The line curving to the left is the main running road! *Mike Vinten/TG*

MILFORD HAVEN: 57XX Class pannier tanks are seen at Milford Haven on 23 January 1962. No 3639 is about to leave on the 2.30pm to Johnston, while No 3654 waits in the loop.

Milford Haven is now reduced to a basic station, with few facilities for passengers, as seen on 20 September 2001. Class 158 No 158871, marked 'Wessex Trains', operates the 11.35 service to Swansea. *Ray Ruffell, courtesy Silver Link Publishing/TG*

MILFORD HAVEN DOCKS were connected to the railway, as seen here in July 1958. The connection no longer exists and the dock area has been 'beautified', as seen in the second photograph. *R. M. Casserley/TG*

NEYLAND (1): This is the end of the line in the late 1950s. A boat yard occupies the foreground in the 2000 view, and part of the station site is occupied by a private house, while the remainder is a public park. *R. S. Carpenter/TG*

NEYLAND (2): This is the approach to the station, with the engine shed in the centre, as seen on 20 September 1962. Goods facilities were withdrawn in December 1963 and passenger services the following June. The station had a succession of names: it opened as Milford Haven, was renamed Neyland in 1859 and New Milford later the same year, before becoming Neyland again in 1906.

The area is now occupied by marine manufacturers and suppliers. With the subsequent building of a bridge over the river, the nearest station to Neyland is now Pembroke Dock rather than Milford Haven. *R. S. Carpenter/TG*

Clynderwen and Clarbeston Road
to Fishguard Harbour

LETTERSTON: The line to Fishguard via Rosebush diverged 1 mile west of Clynderwen, and was opened in stages from 1876. There are very few photographs of this line, as it closed several times before the final withdrawal of passenger services in 1937. A short section at the northern end of the line to Letterston was retained for goods until 1965, and this undated photograph shows the station in early GWR days.

The main buildings still exist, seen here on a wet day in the summer of 2000. The row of houses in the background in the 'past' photograph can just be seen in today's view from the same point. *Lens of Sutton/TG*

WOLF'S CASTLE HALT: Another line was subsequently built from Clarbeston Road to join the original line near Letterston, and this is still used by passenger trains, albeit very infrequently. There were several halts, all of which have been closed. The first was Wolf's Castle Halt, seen here on 8 July 1958 looking toward Fishguard.

The site of the station can still be seen from the former up-side entrance. The overbridge carries the main A40 road to Fishguard. *H. C. Casserley/TG*

WELSH HOOK HALT was another of the halts, and in the distance on 8 July 1958 is a train heading for Fishguard. These halts were only open in daylight hours and even then only on request. Nothing remains today. *H. C. Casserley/TG*

MATHRY ROAD was the first station proper from Clarbeston Road, and on 23 May 1961 a single-coach parcels train bound for Fishguard is approaching; the engine is the last member of the 'Manor' Class, No 7829 *Ramsbury Manor*. The station closed in April 1964 and nothing remains apart from the approach road. *R. Griffiths/TG*

JORDANSTON HALT was the last halt and, like Welsh Hook, had no raised platforms. Not surprisingly there is no trace of the halt itself, although the old halt footpath is still in use for access by track maintenance personnel. All three halts closed on the same day as Mathry Road station. *Lens of Sutton/TG*

FISHGUARD & GOODWICK station is situated in the town of Goodwick, about a mile north-west of Fishguard. The 'past' photograph provides a general view of the station in about 1960.

Despite its convenient location the station closed at the same time as the other intermediate halts and stations in 1964. The former up platform is still intact, and behind the hedge is the main station building. *R. S. Carpenter/TG*

FISHGUARD (GOODWICK) LOCOMOTIVE DEPOT was situated just south of the station on the down side. This 1950s view shows 'Hall' Class No 5908 *Moreton Hall* by the coaling stage. The station is in the background immediately in front of the road overbridge. The shed closed in September 1963 and the site is now an industrial estate. *R. S. Carpenter/TG*

FISHGUARD HARBOUR (1): On 11 June 1960 the 4.25pm to Clarbeston Road is worked by 57XX Class No 7747. The Harbour station buildings are still in use, although no longer exclusively for railway purposes, and there is now only a single platform. *Mike Vinten/TG*

FISHGUARD HARBOUR (2): A good view of the approach to Fishguard Harbour can be obtained from a footbridge leading to the quay. A pannier tank shunts a few box vans in the early 1950s, with the Harbour station in the background beyond the cranes.

All that is left today is the single line from Clarbeston Road, which has been diverted over part of the goods yard site to provide a road entrance to the Harbour on what was the land occupied by the main line. The 'present' photograph, taken in appalling weather in the spring of 2000, shows the only train to run in daylight hours approaching the terminus. The unit is Class 158 No 158864, forming the 12.05 service from Swansea, operated by Wales & West. First Great Western operates the other train, which arrives at 01.10, both connecting with ferries to Rosslare. *R. S. Carpenter/TG*

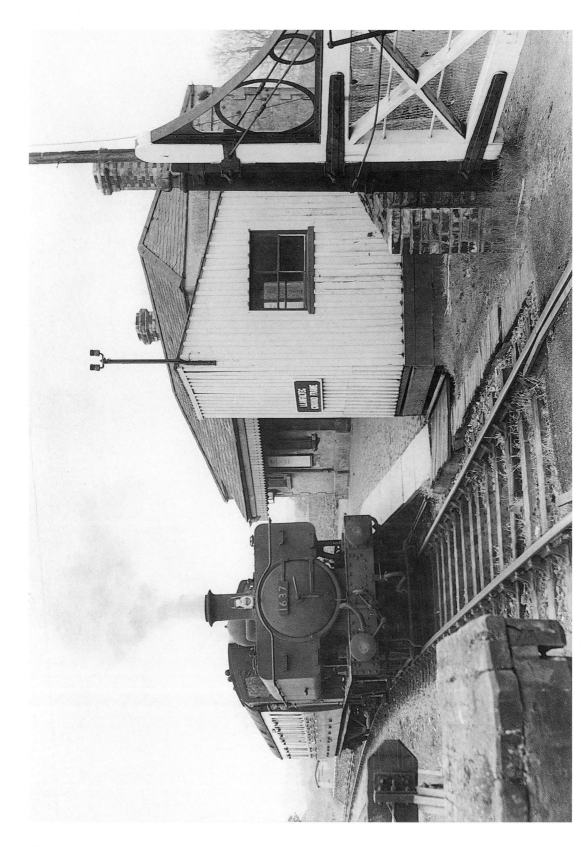

Whitland to Cardigan

LLANFALTEG: The Cardigan branch left the main line at Cardigan Junction, about 2 miles north-west of Whitland. The first station was Llanfalteg, which was 3¾ miles from Whitland and was situated in the centre of the village. A single-coach train bound for Cardigan is seen there on 22 May 1959 hauled by 16XX Class No 1637. The station was erroneously marked as closed on the 1947 Ordnance Survey map, and was downgraded to a halt in the 1950s, together with Login, Rhydowen, Glogue and Kilgerran. The line closed to passengers on 10 September 1962, and nearly 40 years later the site of the station and the level crossing are still readily identifiable. *C. J. Gammell/TG*

LOGIN (1): This was the first station with a substantial main building and served the adjacent village. It is seen here in the early 1960s and the present day; it is now a private residence. *Lens of Sutton/TG*

LOGIN (2): The station was in an isolated area, 3 miles from the nearest main road, and the small communities in the vicinity of this and most of the other intermediate stations on the line never provided the railway with much passenger traffic. These two photographs, looking towards Whitland, were taken 40 years apart. *Lens of Sutton/TG*

LLANGLYDWEN: A Cardigan train, hauled by 45XX Class No 5520, stands in the station on 25 May 1961. Llanglydwen had a passing loop with both lines served by platforms, but passenger trains did not normally cross here.

On 19 July 1960, the date of the second photograph, an up goods train is double-headed by 45XX Class Nos 5549 and 5546, while sister engine No 4557 approaches the station on a passenger train to Cardigan. Today the view of the trackbed from the end of the platform is obscured by trees.

The 6.15pm from Whitland waits for the all clear on 8 July 1958. The single coach is hauled by 16XX Class No 1637.

What was once a picturesque setting has since been turned into something far less attractive, with the coal yard containing hoppers and corrugated buildings. The building on the left identifies the location. *R. G. Griffiths/R. O. Tuck, courtesy Don Gatehouse/R. M. Casserley/TG*

RHYDOWEN had a single platform and passing loop. On 8 July 1958 the gates over the minor road are being opened to road traffic following the departure of a train. The site is now privately owned and there is no trace of the platform. *R. M. Casserley/TG*

LLANFYRNACH had a substantial station building, but no passing loop through the station. The goods yard is behind the camera in this 1958 photograph.

A visit in May 2000 found that the station building was a private residence and the goods yard a fertiliser depot – the roof of the station house is visible beyond the bags. The whole of the area is well kept, in contrast to some other former stations on the line. *R. M. Casserley/TG*

GLOGUE is seen from the level crossing on 8 July 1958; the engine is taking water prior to continuing to Cardigan. The area is now a paddock, with just a few remnants of the platform. *R. M. Casserley/TG*

Another Cardigan train is seen taking water; this time the locomotive is 45XX Class No 4557 on the 4.00pm service from Whitland on 9 June 1960. *Hugh Ballantyne*

CRYMMYCH ARMS (I): In BR days this was the crossing place for the first trains of the day, which left Whitland and Cardigan at 6.20am and 6.50am respectively. 45XX Class No 5520 has the right of way on 25 May 1961.

The station house has been extended and is now a private residence, while the station approach and yard are used for a market and by an agricultural company. *R. Griffiths./TG*

45XX Class No 4557 is working the 10.00am service from Cardigan to Whitland on 11 June 1960. Crymmych Arms station was in the town, which is situated on the main A478 Narberth to Cardigan road. *Mike Vinten*

CRYMMYCH ARMS (2): This more general view looking in the same direction as the picture opposite was taken two years previously. The present view shows the main building and remains of the platform face, but the signal box has been demolished. The road bridge in the background is just visible in both photographs. *H. C. Casserley/TG*

BONCATH (1): The station was on the edge of the town and was provided with a passing loop and two platforms. 16XX Class No 1637 leaves Boncath with a Cardigan train on 10 September 1962. Behind the camera was a level crossing.

Looking in the same direction in May 2000 (*opposite*), the houses glimpsed through the trees in the upper (*present*) photograph are those adjacent to the road overbridge in the background of the 'past' photograph (*above*). The goods yard on the right is partly overgrown, although the approach road is accessible. The station is now within the grounds of a private house and the lower 'present' photograph is a more distant view from the level crossing. *H. R. Newey, courtesy D. K. Jones/TG*

G.W.R.

Boncath

BONCATH (2): The main station building is seen from the train window on 8 July 1958 . The level crossing carries a minor road from the town to the main Cardigan road. All that can be seen in 2000 is shown in the 'present' photograph. *H. C. Casserley/TG*

A similar view of Boncath, taken on 31 May 1959, shows 45XX Class No 4550, a regular to the branch, on the 5.45pm from Cardigan to Whitland. *R. O. Tuck, courtesy Don Gatehouse*

85

KILGERRAN (1) was the last station before Cardigan. In the 'past' view 45XX Class No 5549 calls here on 10 September 1962 on its way to Cardigan. The second view, unobstructed by the train, is looking in the same direction on 8 July 1958. A footpath to the station led from a minor road that passed under the railway at the Cardigan end.

Today there is no trace of the station, but the corrugated building in the goods yard still stands and is in use.
H. R. Newey, courtesy D. K. Jones/R. M. Casserley/TG

G. W. R.

KILGERRAN

KILGERRAN (2): Looking towards Cardigan on 8 July 1958, the trees provide a very good landmark and enable the station site to be located today without any difficulty. *H. C. Casserley/TG*

CARDIGAN (1): This was a pleasant station with a single platform, situated on the opposite bank of the Afon Teifi from the town centre, but still within easy walking distance. 45XX Class No 4557 has recently arrived with the 4.00pm from Whitland on 9 June 1960.

The station building has since been demolished and a new building erected on the site, as seen in May 2000. However, there are remnants of the old platform. *Hugh Ballantyne/TG*

Opposite CARDIGAN (2): Looking towards the buffer stops in 1959, Class 4500 No 4550 is waiting to leave for Whitland. The station site, including the goods shed, is still in use. *R. O. Tuck, courtesy Don Gatehouse/TG*

A similar view taken on 11 June 1960 shows 45XX Class No 4557, this time on the 10.00am to Whitland. In the background is another member of the same Class, No 4550, on a goods train. Goods services were withdrawn in May 1963. *Mike Vinten*

G. W. R.

CARDIGAN

CARDIGAN LOCOMOTIVE DEPOT: There was a small engine shed at Cardigan, as seen on 19 September 1962, the month in which it was closed and passenger services withdrawn. Today a new building stands on the site and is occupied by a removal company. The river is just visible on the extreme right. *R. S. Carpenter/TG*

CARDIGAN (3): A general view of the terminus in 1958 shows No 4556 on the 10.00am train to Whitland and No 4576 on a goods train. The Cardigan bypass has since been built across the station throat and the present-day view is taken from the roadside, of necessity from a slightly different position. *R. M. Casserley/TG*

CARDIGAN (4): The road approach to the station is seen on 8 July 1958. Following closure of the line, the road was improved and additional roads leading to various industrial premises were added. The same location in May 2000 finds that the Morris Oxford car on the left has been displaced by a later version of the same family. *H. C. Casserley/TG*

Carmarthen towards Aberystwyth

BRONWYDD ARMS (1): Travelling north from Carmarthen, the first station on the Aberystwyth line beyond Abergwili Junction (see page 99) is Bronwydd Arms. The first photograph shows Bronwydd Arms on 13 July 1956. The goods yard is surprisingly busy, an indication of the value of the railway to the local rural community. Despite this, goods facilities were withdrawn in December 1963, and passenger services continued until February 1965.

Following closure of the goods yard, the track was removed and all that remained was the running road, as seen in the second view.

The line remained open until 1973, and the station re-opened for passengers in April 1978 under the auspices of the Gwili Railway, which had been founded three years previously. The revitalised station, with the yard relayed, is seen from the same viewpoint in May 2000. *H. C. Casserley/Courtesy Gwili Railway Preservation Society/ TG*

BRONWYDD ARMS (2): These views are looking towards Carmarthen on 13 July 1956 and again on 21 May 2000. The signal box was demolished following closure and the Gwili Railway replaced it with a similar box from Llandebie (see *British Railways Past and Present No 37*). The present-day photograph shows WD 0-6-0 No 71516 *Welsh Guardsman* on a train to Llwyfan Cerrig. *H. C. Casserley/TG*

CONWIL (1): Both Bronwydd Arms and the next station of Conwil are close to the main A484 road from Carmarthen to Cardigan. This is the approach to Conwil on 13 July 1956 and 21 May 2000, both visits being made in poor weather. Some of the track is still in place today, although hidden in the undergrowth, and the sidings to the right contain rolling-stock belonging to the Gwili Railway. *H. C. Casserley/TG*

CONWIL (2): This is the view looking north on the same two dates. Note the different station name spellings, the longer also used on a mock GWR platform ticket issued by the Gwili Railway. The line north of the next station of Llanpumpsaint is covered in *British Railways Past and Present No 32*. *H. C. Casserley/TG*

S.1 Great Western Railway M∙V

CYNWYL ELFED

ADMIT ONE to Platform 1d

This Ticket must be given up on leaving Platform
Available one hour. For conditions see back. p.m

3600

Carmarthen to Llandilo

ABERGWILI: The LNWR line to Llandilo left the Aberystwyth line at Abergwili Junction, and after crossing the Afon Gwili arrived at Abergwili station. This is the view looking towards the junction on 8 August 1962, with a train bound for Carmarthen in the distance.

A new Carmarthen bypass and associated roads have transformed the area and the trackbed has been obliterated. However, careful study of old and new maps and the fields in the background enabled the station site to be located in May 2000. *C. J. Gammell/TG*

NANTGAREDIG: The line follows the Afon Tywi all the way to Llandilo. Trains were photographed crossing at the next station of Nantgaredig on the evening of 8 June 1960: 57XX Class No 9606 is working the 6.10pm from Carmarthen to Llandilo, and in the opposite direction is the tail of the 6.10pm from Llandilo. In contrast to Abergwili, this station site was easy to locate, as the station name is still displayed. The only confusion was that the building is now two storeys high. *Hugh Ballantyne/TG*

LLANARTHNEY: A train bound for Llandilo on 8 August 1960, hauled by Class 7400 No 7440, has just left two passengers for the walk along the lane to the village. The station is now a private residence and the trackbed on private land. *C. J. Gammell/TG*

DRYSLLWYN station was located close to a castle of the same name. The view looking east in 1962 was very similar to that at Abergwili looking west. Today's view is much more restricted, but very pleasant. The station is now a private residence and the platform forms part of the garden. Note the 'narrow gauge' track in the foreground. *C. J. Gammell/TG*

GOLDEN GROVE was another station close to the river, but about a mile from the village. On 8 August 1962 a Llandilo to Carmarthen train waits for permission to enter the next single-line section.

In May 2000 the station and trackbed were readily recognisable, and in common with several of the other stations on the line, the station building is in use as a private dwelling house. *C. J. Gammell/TG*

LLANDILO BRIDGE: No 7440 is seen again, this time at Llandilo Bridge, the last station before the junction with the Central Wales Line. This station was very close to Ffairfach and only three-quarters of a mile from Llandilo. A visit in 2000 found that nothing remained of the platform or trackbed. *C. J. Gammell/TG*

Carmarthen toward Llanelly

CARMARTHEN JUNCTION: Carmarthen's original station was located further south than the present station at what later became the junction of the main line and the line to the present station. The original station became known as Carmarthen Junction and the new station Carmarthen Town. Junction station closed in 1926 and Town station became plain Carmarthen. This early photograph shows Carmarthen Junction station to be well appointed.

On 18 May 2000 Class 158 No 158827 approaches the site of Junction station forming the 08.35 Milford Haven to Swansea service. The station site is occupied by a large warehouse built right up to the platform edge. *Lens of Sutton/TG*

FERRYSIDE was, as the name implies, situated by a river, the Afon Tywi. Judging by the crowds on the platform in this early photograph, this must have been a special train.

The post-steam era shot from the same viewpoint shows a Carmarthen-bound DMU on 4 June 1963. Ferryside later became an unstaffed request stop, and is still open, complete with semaphore signals, and has a service every day of the week. *Lens of Sutton/Adrian Vaughan/TG*

S W R

Chepstow to

Ferryside

KIDWELLY: Looking towards Llanelly, this is the station in GWR days, probably in the 1930s. Kidwelly is also still open, and the 10.05 Swansea to Pembroke Dock service is not scheduled to stop (even by request) and passes through on 18 May 2000 formed of Class 158 No 158867 in new livery. *Lens of Sutton/TG*

KIDWELLY FLATS HALT was built between Kidwelly and Burry Port during the Second World War, and the 'past' photograph shows the partly demolished platform in the 1960s, the halt having closed in the late 1950s. It was built to serve a nearby air base, which later became a motor sports centre. No trace of the halt remains. *Lens of Sutton/TG*

PEMBREY & BURRY PORT station is seen at the turn of the century, with a Swansea-bound train. It is amazing how little the immediate environment has changed: most of the shops and houses still exist, as does the footbridge. The station is still open and stops are mandatory. On 18 May 2000 Class 153 No 153370, forming the 12.11 Swansea to Tenby service, has just collected a few passengers. *Lens of Sutton/TG*

The view from the footbridge at Pembrey & Burry Port on 21 May 1958 shows 51XX Class No 4122 on the 7.00pm from Swansea to Pembroke Dock. This was the interchange station for the service to Cwm Mawr of the Burry Port & Gwendraeth Valley Railway (BPGVR), which became part of the GWR at the 1923 Grouping. Stations east of Pembrey & Burry Port from Llanelly towards Swansea and beyond are covered in *British Railways Past and Present No 37*. *N. C. Simmons, courtesy Hugh Davies*

Burry Port to Cwm Mawr

BURRY PORT (1): The Burry Port & Gwendraeth Valley Railway (BPGVR) station was adjacent to the main-line station, and was known as plain Burry Port. A train for Cwm Mawr headed by 16XX Class No 1609 is seen there about 1950. Note the low-roofed carriages, necessary to pass under the main-line bridge. In contrast to the GWR station, the BPGVR site has changed almost out of recognition. The area is very flat and there are few identifying features to link 'past' and 'present'. However, the station site is easy to find as there are still remnants of the platform, and in the background the Neptune Hotel has become Neptune's Palace. At the time of writing it was up for sale. *R. W. A. Jones, courtesy Don Gatehouse/TG*

There were extensive yards just east of the station, which handled large amounts of coal traffic. Former BPGVR No 12, later GWR No 2165, was photographed by the author on his first visit to Burry Port on 9 August 1954. This engine was withdrawn the following year. *TG*

BURRY PORT (2): Passenger serves ceased in September 1953, but coal trains continued to run until a re-instated connection was made with the main line near Kidwelly, which is still extant but out of use. This resulted in closure of the yard at Burry Port. On 7 September 1983, shortly before closure, three Class 03 locomotives are seen at Burry Port. The train of coal wagons is double-headed by Nos 03119 and 03141,while in the background is No 03152. Short lengths of track and the stone building in the background confirmed the location on a visit in 2000. *Hugh Ballantyne/TG*

BURRY PORT LOCOMOTIVE SHED: This general view of the engine shed area on 21 September 1962 shows a Class 03 shunter in the background, while a desolate scene greeted the author on his 2000 visit. *R. S. Carpenter/TG*

Outside Burry Port engine shed on 17 April 1949 was another ex-BPGVR engine, No 2167, and 1901 Class pannier tank No 2019. *W. Potter, courtesy Don Gatehouse*

BURRY PORT (3): Another view of the coal train on 7 September 1983, leaving for Coed Bach and Cwm Mawr. Carmarthen Bay power station closed the same year, thus depriving the photographer of a landmark and backdrop for the present-day view, although the house immediately to the left of the power station acts as a marker. The BPGVR line passed under the main line at a point just behind the camera and this also helped to identify the correct location. *Hugh Ballantyne/TG*

PEMBREY HALT: The village of Pembrey is a mile west of Burry Port and the BPGVR provided a halt there. The first photograph shows the halt in 1957, four years after closure.

Following the opening of the connection to the branch near Kidwelly in 1983, the track on the abandoned section of line was removed, and the 'present' photograph shows the site of Pembrey Halt today. *Adrian Vaughan/TG*

COED BACH COAL WASHERY was located near the intersection of the lines from Burry Port and Kidwelly, and Class 08 No 08994 *Gwendraeth* is shunting there on 10 January 1989. This and all the other diesel locomotives using the BPGVR line had cut-down cabs because of limited clearances.

The washery has since closed and been demolished, and the only building still standing is the hut on the extreme left-hand side of both photographs. *Hugh Ballantyne/TG*

PONTYATES (1): A railway enthusiasts' special was run on the BPGVR on 25 September 1965, and is seen here at Pontyates returning from Cwm Mawr behind 16XX Class No 1669.

The station has now gone and the level crossing gates have been replaced. However, the track is still in place, perhaps on the optimistic assumption that one day coal traffic will return. *Mike Vinten/TG*

A view from the other end of Pontyates station on 21 May 1958 before it was demolished. *Norman Simmons courtesy Hugh Davies*

PONTYBEREM station was also photographed on 21 May 1958, looking toward Burry Port. In the second view, taken in September 1983, a coal train double-headed by Class 03 Nos 03119 and 03141 heads for Cwm Mawr.

The present-day view of Pontyberem has changed little. The 'Beware of Trains' sign features in all three photographs.
Hugh Ballantyne/TG

CWM MAWR: The end of the line – Cwm Mawr station with 16XX Class pannier tank No 1609 taking water prior to returning with its train to Burry Port about 1950.

The platform, water tower, signal box and even the track have been removed. Other buildings in the immediate vicinity were still in use at the time of the author's visit in 2000. *R. W. A. Jones, courtesy Don Gatehouse/TG*

INDEX OF LOCATIONS